GUIDE FOR

BARNDOMINIUM HOUSE PLAN

A Complete Walkthrough on How to Build Your Barndominium House

Olanipekun Segun

Contents

INTRODUCTION 5

Chapter 1: Welcome To Barndominium 6

What Makes A House A Barndominium?............ 8

How Does A Barndominium Appear?.................. 9

CHAPTER 2: WHY BARNDOMINIUM ARE SO POPULAR... 12

Characteristics Of Barndominium 12

Barndominium Advantages Save Your Money 15

Work Smarter Not Harder.................................... 15

Safer Vs Fire & Weather.......................................16

CHAPTER 3: HOW DID BARNDOMINIUM KITS WORK?.. 18

Barndominium Home With Endless Potential... 20

Engineered Easy To Assemble............................. 21

Concrete & Foundation Requirement.................. 21

CHAPTER 4: THE INTERIOR AND EXTERIOR DESIGN TOUR..25

Your Barndominium/Home Kit Designing......... 27

The Exterior Custom.. 30

CHAPTER 5: HOW COSTLY IT'S TO BUILD A BARNDOMINIUM? 32

How Costly It's To Renovated Barns? 35

Conclusion 37

INTRODUCTION

The barndominium is a perfect example of how the past can inspire the present. This architectural design may seem novel on home remodeling and decorating television shows, yet it has been popular in rural areas for quite some time.

A barndominium was about more than simply looks, though. It was all about making a house that was truly yours, one that reflected your tastes and your character.

This book will surely guide you to incorporate sustainable materials and energy-efficient features throughout the entire house, from scratch to the roof. If you wanted to create a home that was not only beautiful but also eco-friendly and kind to the environment.

Even before the barndominium became a trend in this generation, they were the ultimate in live-work spaces. They were a must-have for families who subsisted on farming and other forms of self-sufficiency, such as blacksmithing and the production of handcrafted goods like cheeses, in the past.

Chapter 1: Welcome To Barndominium

A barndominium is a type of multi-use building that combines living quarters for a family with a huge garage or workshop allowing the owner to pursue a hobby or make a living.

Most of these homes started off as barn conversions, but there are only so many old barns to use. Even without the difficulty of making old utilitarian livestock buildings healthy and safe to live in, there are return-on-investment issues for transforming them into modern family residences.

Normally, barndominium kits, or the shell kits, use a simple rectangular layout, allowing total flexibility for interior floor plans. This flexibility is a big draw, as is the openness.

High, vaulted ceilings are common, and so are steel-frame buildings. Barndominiums are one of the residential housing

Trends with the highest rate of growth. Essentially, they are converted barns or barn-shaped buildings erected from scratch, typically composed of metal or wood. By blending some of the structural elements of agrarian buildings with up market accents of contemporary design, these structures create an unusual blend of country and urban architecture.

According to some home Top Agent Research Insights for Summer 2022, buyer interest in barndominium has increased over the previous two years, in part because of style and in part due to price and quicker construction. Especially in rural regions away from the coasts, such as Texas, Montana, and Tennessee, they are becoming an increasingly popular option for single-family homes.

So, do you wish to participate in the barndominium trend? and this home design suitable for you? Let's raise the roof rafters and show all the relevant information regarding barndominiums.

What Makes A House A Barndominium?

You might think of a barndominium as a cross between a barn and a condo. The two primary categories   are:

The converted barn is a real agricultural building once used for storing food, cattle, or equipment.

Although a barn may have served as inspiration for this new structure, a barn was never its intended use.

It's basically a carbon copy of the revised edition in terms of design and format.

Although the term "barn conversion" was first used to describe structures that had previously served as barns, the new-construction variant is now the norm. The proper classification of barndominiums is a matter of some debate, bordering on a theological conflict.

There are many who insist that a building cannot be considered a barndominium if it features any wood. But don't let yourself become obsessed. Howe considers a building to be a barndominium if it has a metal exterior and is built in the barndo style.

How Does A Barndominium Appear?

So, how would you like it to appear? The huge rectangular shape is the most distinguishing feature they share. What is the size? That is entirely up to your preferences and financial limitations.

After that, it's down to personal preference, practical considerations, and the way you want to spend your time at home.

Construction of a new-from-scratch barndominium extremely pleasant When you use steel for the structure's skeleton, you also receive metal walls and a metal roof (if you want them). (Of course, an all-metal exterior is the best option due to its lifespan, durability, affordability, little maintenance, and high security.)

How would you like the design to look? What's that, you say? Done! Do the drawing. A roomy loft, ideal for use as a study or hangout for the whole family? Okay. Incorporate it into your plans. With plenty of strategically located windows, you can take advantage of the sun all year. Then, incorporate them into your drawings.

Making decisions is the most challenging aspect of constructing a barndominium. It can be downright scary for some people, which is why it's helpful to have design assistance for details you might miss.

After all, you have complete control over every aperture, door, and crevice at your disposal.

CHAPTER 2: WHY BARNDOMINIUM ARE SO POPULAR

Do you notice that "people don't need horses in the living room these days, so that's obviously not why barndominiums are popular," you're right.

Sometimes, we do think barndominiums are popular for a few reasons. The flexibility mentioned earlier, that's phenomenal, for starters. Why because you have struggled to accommodate your work-at-home business in a home that doesn't work for you, when you can build a barndominium beautiful designed around all your work-life needs, in a setting you love?

Characteristics Of Barndominium

Possibility, flexibility, adaptability – these are the hallmarks of great barndominiums. Ideally, they're custom-built with the homeowner in mind – from how they like to relax through to their work-life requirements. Here are a few factors fueling the barndominium trend:

Availability, all-in building **costs are incredibly attractive.**

Simple-looking exteriors design can be deceptive; inside, they tend to have **high ceilings, airy interiors, and enviable light.**

Often constructed from wooden or metal frames and even metal and wooden panel exteriors, **these homes need little maintenance,** allowing homeowners to forget about things like structural pest infestations, frame rot, or needing to paint the exterior every 5 to 10 years.

Engineered to be **safe in storm-prone regions** with high winds, threats of wildfire, and large snow loads.

Metal and wooden structures can **lower energy costs** when done right (and we've got tips for that, too – not to mention our metal roofs are great for solar panel arrays).

Insurance rates can be lower as well thanks to wind-resistance, fire-resistance, and other durability factors with metal-framed homes.

Great custom floor plans can mean enjoying the protection of modern engineered metal/wooden-frame construction while retaining rustic charm.

Barndominium Kits: Build Your Dream Home

Barndominium with Absolute Steel Kits, building your dream home can be easier and more inexpensive than you ever thought possible. Building your home is potentially the biggest investment you'll ever make, but what if you could build for thousands less than a conventional site built home? Well, you can, with our barndominium kits.

A barndominium is a live-work space, a space big enough for both a family home and a workshop or large garage area, where the homeowner works on their passion or their livelihood.

Barndominium Advantages Save Your Money

You can get the dream home you want with a custom-made barndominium kit from kitchen cupboards to skylights, a barndominium kit features the same easy flexibility of a steel building kit. It goes together easily with everyday tools, whether you're a mastermind or someone learning the ropes. Substantially more affordable, a barndominium kit are simple – and the more you do yourself, the more money you save.

Work Smarter Not Harder

The Work from home allows you to end your work commute. That means lower gas costs, less vehicle wear-and-tear, fewer daily expenses. But it also means more time to live life on your terms. How much time have you spent commuting monthly? How much stress have you experience from bad traffic, heavy weather, and unavoidable delays? What could you do with those extra 40, 50, 60 or more hours per month? What would you rather spend your gas money on?

Safer Vs Fire & Weather

Buildings with metal paneling often survive wild land fires, since they're fire resistant. Metal barndominium shells can be engineered to withstand 160-mile-an-hour sustained winds when erected with proper concrete footings, which can last for between 20 to 45 years against peeling, fading, and chalking. Same goes with the metal roofs. You can use the fabricated to be some of the lightest, strongest roofs for modern homes, ideal for heavy snow.

People desire housing, yet building takes time. Due to their pole construction method, but I can assure you that building a barndominium takes less time.

In addition to being constructed rapidly and affordably, barndos are less expensive than standard single-family dwellings. Even with new construction, a barndominium might be less expensive per square foot than a regular home.

This is owing to the steel exterior, which reduces the cost of aesthetic design elements such as brick or roof shingles. It also reduces maintenance costs, as steel is much easier to maintain than materials used in conventional housing construction. As a result, homeowners may also benefit from lower insurance premiums. As a result of the materials being less expensive, the building's insurance costs might be reduced.

Another reason for the popularity of barndominium is that their construction is more eco-friendly than those of many traditional residences. New versions can also be constructed to be energy-efficient by sealing the structure, installing double-paned windows, and spraying foam insulation.

CHAPTER 3: HOW DID BARNDOMINIUM KITS WORK?

This starts with the shell. Pick from line of existing barndominium designs, the metal or wooden frame size and style for the building, or come up with a design of your own. You're the manufacturer; you can execute your vision, so your home is exactly what you want it to be. You can build the steel frame, and you can also create any style paneling your window/door build to your own standard requirement.

The interior design is all about you. Designing the floor plan your way. No matter what your vision is, the floor plan can fit your lifestyle. Build with wood studs or order metal framing. And you'll have so many choices to make – every doorknob, nook, and cranny will be decided by you. So will the wall placement – or the lack thereof if you're looking for an open design.

Materials, contractors, and products are all your choice. Think of yourself as the general contractor. You're the boss here. You control the subcontractors – or you do it yourself, whatever you like.

In some areas you can hire local contractors. If you want to fly solo and find your own providers and professionals, or are dead set on doing it all yourself, it's all good with Absolute Steel. However you do it.

Barndominium Home With Endless Potential

The brilliant thing about the barndominium kits made by Absolute Steel is that they can be anything you want.

Your engineers and fabricators will construct to your design, making on-site assembly quick and simple, whether you choose one of our conventional building configurations or create something entirely new from scratch.

Particularly when working with a limited budget, home construction benefits greatly from adaptability. Interiors can be designed cheaply to save money, then upgraded as funds become available.

For instance, if you are on a tight budget, you could use polished concrete slabs for flooring and countertops for a few years before upgrading to hardwood and marble. Instead of worrying about expensive worktops or flooring if money is tight, consider upgrading to a somewhat larger room with the greatest windows you can afford.

You'll have plenty of time to settle in and make the house your own during the next few decades.

Engineered Easy To Assemble

Your kit home's finished shell can be put together by as few as two people, with little or no prior construction experience and using common tools! This means YOU can do it, whether you build yourself or act as an owner/builder using local tradesmen and contractors.

Concrete & Foundation Requirement

For Barndominium And Kit Homes

Absolute Steel barndominiums and kit homes are designed to be anchored to a concrete footing or slab.

While technically, our buildings can be installed on bare earth, because someone will be living in the barndominium or kit home local building codes will apply. Those building codes will require a concrete footing or slab.

Note for Cold Climates: The below-mentioned concrete uses do not take into consideration frost line necessities. Your concrete footings will need to be dug deeper than shown in this diagram if you are in a region with severe winters and a frost line. The frost line criteria for your location can be obtained from your local building authorities.

Mounting On A Concrete Slab

Always double-check the concrete specifications with your local building department. An engineer can be contracted if necessary. Please note that the details provided below are generic in nature and may not apply to your unique region at all.

Size Of Slats

The length of your slab should be 2 inches more than the breadth of your structure. If you have a building that is 20 feet broad and 40 feet long, your slab should be 20 feet wide and 40 feet, two inches long.

Thickness of a slab

A 4-inch-thick floor is recommended. There needs to be a minimum of 2500 psi of strength in the concrete, and either fiber mesh reinforcement added at the batch plant or #3 rebar on 24" centers.

The slab should be at least 6 inches thick, and 4000-psi concrete should be used if you intend to park trucks or large recreational vehicles (RVs) within. This isn't necessary for a kit house, but a barndominium's garage space is perfect for storing cars and tractors.

Expansion joints in the slab should be either saw-cut immediately after the concrete has been poured or toweled in during the concrete finishing process.

Footing Requirement

At the same time as your slab is poured, you will also need to pour **perimeter footings**, as illustrated below. This is called a *monolithic pour* or *monolithic slab*.

Perimeter footings should be 12″ wide, and 12″ deep. (Deeper in the event you are contending with a frost line) You can include the 4″ slab thickness in the 12″ total depth; in other words, the footing would extend 8″ below the slab. As shown in the detail drawings, your footings will also need continuous runs of #4 rebar along the top and bottom.

In our local area, footings of this type would cost approximately $16.50 per lineal (running) foot.

CHAPTER 4: THE INTERIOR AND EXTERIOR DESIGN TOUR

As you ascend the cedar-wrapped porch steps, the sturdy and energy-saving features of this barndominium give way to a luxurious mountain hideaway. Once you pass through the heavenly blue door, you'll be able to take in the many luxurious touches throughout the building.

The high-end laminate flooring, metal ceilings, and tongue-and-groove stained pine walls are only the beginning. This home's quality and care for detail are evident in the handmade mountain theme barn door, concrete countertops, Amish-made cabinets, and stainless steel appliances.

Then look out the elevated window wrapped great room which offers a near 180 degree view of the mountains. Beyond the over sized master bedroom and other two bedrooms with ample closet space, this home offers other spaces for the way people live today. The roomy mudroom off the entry provides a place to drop off shoes, jackets or hiking gear at the end of a long day. It also has room for shelving for a pantry.

The office provides a place to work at home which seems to be not just a trend but the way people will live for the foreseeable future. The spacious laundry room offers not just a place to do laundry but offers lots of additional storage with access to the crawl space that provides additional conditioned space for storage. The two bathrooms are equally well appointed with granite sink bases, beautiful custom ceramic tile and choice of either a bath or a shower.

Your Barndominium/Home Kit Designing
General Layout and Building Size

You can figure out what building dimensions you'd like. This might come after you decide how much square footage you want.

Once you have your square footage amount, work that into a rectangle/square dimension (our square foot price varies depending on your building size & design). Example: You want a 2000 square foot building. That could either be a 40' x 50' or a 20' x 100'.

Once you have your dimensions figured out, start thinking about your wall height. Do you want 16' tall, vaulted ceilings with loft space or would you prefer a modest 10' tall sidewall single story with enough height to have a comfortable ceiling that you can run ventilation through?

Do you want any overhangs now that you have all the measurements you need? If so, would they be located on the eave sides or gable ends? What is your desired leg height, and how far away from the wall would you like the overhang to be?

Frame-Outs

Now that you have performed the aforementioned steps and determined your desired dimensions, you may turn your attention to the external frame-outs (single pedestrian door frame-outs, double pedestrian door frame-outs, window frame-outs, and garage door frame-outs).

After settling on the total number of external frame-outs you desire, it is time to settle on the exact measurements of those openings. Our normal window frame-out size is 3' x 3', and our standard frame-out size for pedestrian doors is 3' wide by 6' 8" high, but we can accommodate unique sizes for the windows and doors you want.

If you decide to go with garage door frame-outs, you'll also need to specify their width and height. Keep in mind that the height of your garage door may need to be higher than the height of your walls by up to 2 feet.

Snow and Wind Loads

Be familiar with the local specifications for snow and wind loads. Contacting the local building department will provide you with that data.

Remember these maximums when designing the frame for your Absolute Steel barndominium:

In terms of gable width, the maximum allowed is 42 feet. Remember that you can make your structure longer by connecting lean-tos to the eave sides.

Maximum Wall Height (feet): 16

No Maximum Length Restriction

Superior Yield Strength From A Paint Finish That Last Forever

The highest yield strength of sheet metal is a measure of its stress tolerance. A material's grade is based on the point at which it sustains permanent strain, also known as the point at which it begins to give or go plastic, during testing.

The Exterior Custom

Great as steel's advantages are, you may have your heart set on something different for your home's exterior walls. That's why you can an expert that will give you choice of many different exterior treatments.

From shakes, shingles or shiplap, to stone, stucco or brick and beyond, the selection is wide open.

CHAPTER 5: HOW COSTLY IT'S TO BUILD A BARNDOMINIUM?

The expense of converting a barn into a home was relatively low — abandoned barns can sell for less than houses and offer ample room for modification and repurposing — barndominiums became initially popular. However, there are a limited number of barns available, and they are restricted to select regions. If you desire a barndominium on your terms and in your ideal location, you will likely need to construct one.

There are two methods for constructing a barndominium: There are kits that offer you with the necessary materials to construct a construction in a predetermined style, as well as the opportunity to build anything from scratch.

You will still be responsible for much of the material outside of the frame as well as the labor to put everything together, which might add significant expense or require a great deal of expertise. If you engage a contractor, you can anticipate their labor to account for up to 20 percent of the entire cost of the project.

You may also opt for a completely bespoke design. According to HomeAdvisor, you should anticipate to pay between $94 and $120 per square foot. This might cost you more than $500,000 total. This is less expensive than the cost of constructing a conventional home, but it is not inexpensive.

HomeAdvisor estimates that a barndominium costs between $94 and $120 per square foot, depending on the finishes you choose and the cost of labor in your location. Typically, the cost per square foot to build a home is from $100 to $200.

Howe observes that, due to the fluctuating costs of building materials and labor, a lot depends on the market and the resources available at the moment. Accordingly, you can anticipate that building a barndominium will be anywhere from 10 to 40 percent less expensive than building a conventional home.

How Costly It's To Renovated Barns?

Compared to constructing a new barndominium, it may be less expensive to find an existing barn and convert it into a residence.

The cost will vary greatly based on the size of the barn, the amount of work required for the conversion, and your specific goals for the residence. The average cost of conversion, according to the website House Digest, is approximately $30,000.

Despite the fact that this may appear inexpensive, it is a substantial undertaking. When converting a barn, homeowners must factor in the time and cost of installing concrete floors, plumbing and electrical wiring, and heating and cooling systems. Location is frequently the decisive factor between building a new barn and adapting an existing one, so many purchasers who desire a bardominium will need to consider a new construction.

Conclusion

Some say these building styles go back to ancient housing needs, especially in places like Northern Europe, with harsh climates and punishing winters. It was common for families to need to over winter their livestock in their homes, to keep them healthy and alive through to spring. There'd often be a stable on the main floor for valuable livestock and family living quarters above.

Printed in the USA
CPSIA information can be obtained
at www.ICGtesting.com
CBHW022202020924
13996CB00015B/101